LC 6/24/04

superstars!
superstars!
superstars!

CREATIVE EDUCATION SPORTS SUPERSTARS

dave cowens

by Robert Armstrong

photographs by Bruce Curtis

CREATIVE EDUCATION
CHILDRENS PRESS

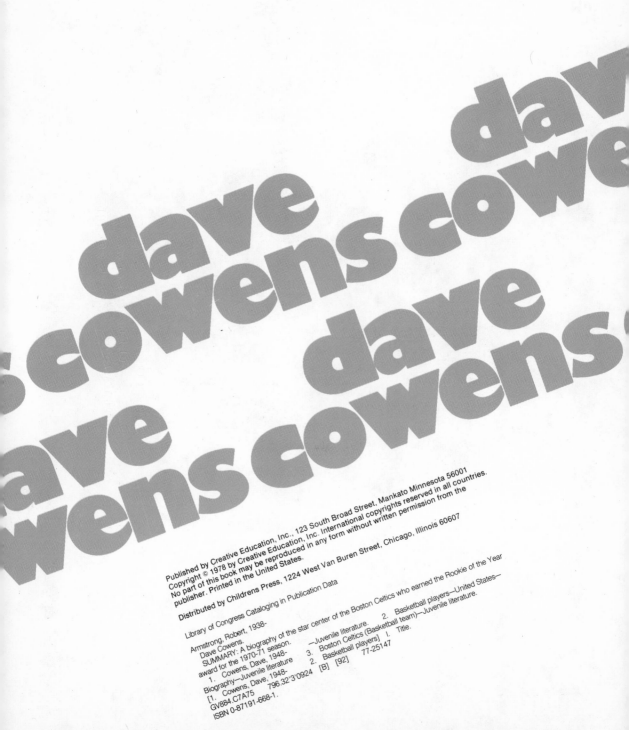

Published by Creative Education, Inc., 123 South Broad Street, Mankato Minnesota 56001
Copyright © 1978 by Creative Education, Inc. International copyrights reserved in all countries.
No part of this book may be reproduced in any form without written permission from the
publisher. Printed in the United States.

Distributed by Childrens Press, 1224 West Van Buren Street, Chicago, Illinois 60607

Library of Congress Cataloging in Publication Data

Armstrong, Robert, 1938-
    Dave Cowens.
    SUMMARY: A biography of the star center of the Boston Celtics who earned the Rookie of the Year
award for the 1970-71 season.
    1.   Cowens, Dave, 1948-   —Juvenile literature.   2.   Basketball players—United States—
Biography—Juvenile literature   3.   Boston Celtics (Basketball team)—Juvenile literature.
    [1.   Cowens, Dave, 1948-   2.   Basketball players]   I.   Title.
GV884.C7A75   796.32'3'0924   [B]   [92]   77-25147
ISBN 0-87191-668-1.

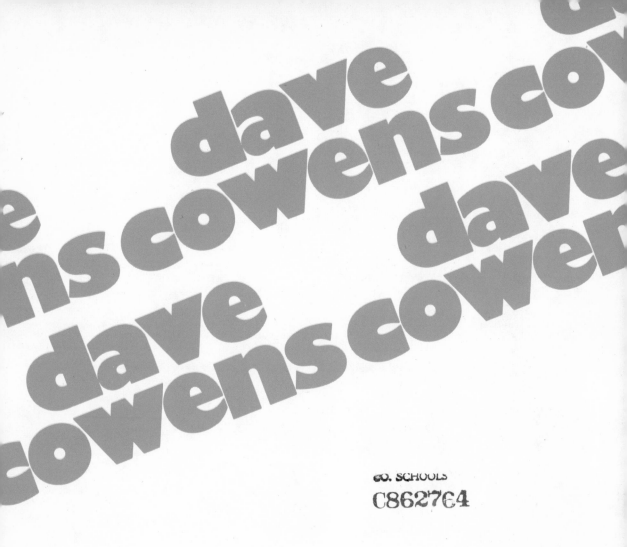

Perhaps only another redhead would have understood.

There was Dave Cowens saying he'd had enough. He was the star center of the Boston Celtics. The team was the defending National Basketball Association (NBA) champions. The six-foot, nine-inch center said he needed a rest.

The 1976-1977 season was only eight games old when Dave Cowens said he wanted out. Maybe next year he'd come back. Maybe never. He'd have to see how things worked out.

The basketball world was stunned. It shouldn't have been. Dave had proven himself to be anything but one of the crowd during his six years in the NBA. He is fiery, stubborn, determined, impulsive. He is also a perfectionist.

Cowens is one of the best centers in the pro game. Check that. He is one of the best players in the game . . . at any position.

This is true not merely because Dave scores a lot of points or grabs plenty of rebounds or plays good defense. He does score and rebound and is a master at defense. Rather, it is because he is totally dedicated to

Boston's team concept of basketball. This concept requires almost total unselfishness if it is to work.

That dedication and his desire for perfection led to his November 1976 escapade. It was an era famous for its pampered, temperamental, very-high-paid athletes. Many of them thought they earned their salaries just by showing up.

In this era, Dave Cowens seemed almost too good to be true. He wanted to get away because he felt he was not earning his paycheck. He is reportedly paid $280,000 a year.

When he left, Dave was averaging over 18 points a game. He was pulling down 15 rebounds a game. He was playing 39 of a game's 48 minutes. Then, suddenly, he made his blockbuster announcement. His audience was Red Auerbach, the Celtics' general manager.

"I just wasn't making a contribution or helping the team." That's what Cowens later told a Boston reporter. "I had no motivation or enthusiasm. It just got to a point where I felt guilty taking my salary." He said at the time that he "might get the urge to return and play basketball the way I should play it." He believed he was not playing that way when he left.

"I know a lot of people will think I'm a fool," Cowens told the reporter. "I don't think I've done anything wrong."

Right now he wanted "to do all the things I haven't been able to do over the last 10 years."

The Celtics' reaction to Dave's announcement was surprising. It was mild and calm. Perhaps this is because the adjective "wily" must have been invented for Red Auerbach. He has long been respected as one of the smartest men in pro basketball. Auerbach had led the team to what seemed like its first hundred or so NBA titles.

It was also Auerbach, then general manager, who saw Dave's possibilities. Red plucked Dave out of the college ranks in 1970. Others had passed over Dave. They didn't think he was tall enough for a good pro center.

Auerbach had a reputation for being explosive. Maybe he was even more explosive than his superstar center. But when the news came, there was no explosion. No fines were announced. Dave was not criticized.

Auerbach merely talked to the press on November 10. He said that Dave was being given "a leave of absence for an indefinite period." The leave was "for personal reasons."

Reporters asked Auerbach if Cowens might be gone a week, a month, or longer. "I can't tell," Auerbach said. "The only person who knows that is Dave." Auerbach noted that he had been in pro basketball for 30 years. "This is the first time anything like this has happened."

No one should have been surprised that Cowens was responsible for another first. He had been establishing firsts since his rookie year in the NBA. That was the 1970-1971 season. Perhaps his most important contribution was the way he played center. He changed the whole way of thinking about how it could be played.

The center in pro basketball had been a stationary position. It was usually played by a big, often rather immobile man. His main roles were to score points and to rebound.

Dave first, then Bob McAdoo a little later, changed this approach. They proved a team could win if the center moved all over the court. This opened up a new way of approaching the offense. Of course you had to have a. center with Dave Cowens' ability.Maybe the most impressive thing about Dave Cowens is that he can play center either way.

Sometimes Cowens will play against a giant like Kareem Abdul-Jabbar. Some say the Lakers' star is 7-feet, 4-inches tall. Against Abdul-Jabbar Cowens can move outside. He can shoot 20-foot jump shots with accuracy. That creates a special problem for Abdul-Jabbar. He can come outside to guard Dave. If he does, he leaves the

lane open. Other Celtics can take a pass from Cowens and drive to the unprotected basket. Abdul-Jabbar's other choice is to stay close to the basket. This leaves Cowens with open shots. Either way the Celtics gain something.

Artis Gilmore is built very much along the same lines as Abdul-Jabbar. Gilmore is the Chicago Bulls' center. He was a superstar in the American Basketball Association (ABA). Then the younger league merged with the NBA in 1976. Gilmore went to Chicago. He has described the problems a center such as Cowens poses for him.

''The toughest centers for me to play are the ones who shoot well from outside. You have to move away from the basket to contest the shot. Then you're leaving room for somebody to get in behind you.'' Gilmore noted that this also hurts your rebounding. The rebound may be already off the board when you return to the basket.

Cowens can also play center the way it is usually played. He has a powerful inside game against a smaller, more mobile player. The New York Knicks' McAdoo would be an example. Dave normally weighs 230 pounds. He uses his size and strength. He can move a player such as McAdoo to the basket. Here Dave can overpower the rival center.

Dave's value to the Celtics is not limited to offense. He was named to the NBA's All-Defensive team for the first time in 1975-1976. This is particularly notable. The Celtics rely on team defense. Each player helps one another under this concept. It is more difficult for one player to stand out. On defense, Dave is strong enough to guard even the biggest center. He is quick enough to switch over to a forward or guard in an emergency.

"The center," Cowens has said, "is the quarterback of the defense. He must see everything that's happening. He must call out the picks. He must be ready to help out if someone else's man gets free."

Cowens at that time talked about playing against Abdul-Jabbar or Tommy Burleson, another seven-footer. "I play percentages. I try to make it as tough as possible for them to get the position they want to get.

"Most of them want to set down low on you. You want to keep them as far away from the basket as possible. You have to use your quickness to do that. You want to make them get the ball further out than they like. Then, most times, they won't be in shooting range for their hook shots.

"They are still going to make their shots. But you can hold them from doing what they want to do when they want to do it. Then, too, you try to tire them out. You run them and make them pay the price."

Dave also excels in rebounding. He is a good jumper. However, that's not what accounts for his rebounding success. He can't outjump Abdul-Jabbar, Gilmore, or Seattle's Burleson. All are five or more inches taller than Cowens.

He rebounds with the huge centers because he has mastered the art of playing position basketball. This involves blocking rival centers away from the backboards. Once he does this, he can use his jumping ability. This, plus his strength and quickness, make him one of the league's top rebounders.

Dave's coach, Tom Heinsohn, has talked about when Dave "goes up in the air" to rebound. "He takes up an incredible amount of space. He takes up about as much as Bill Russell used to occupy."

The Celtics at first had one problem with Cowens. They didn't know where to play him. Should he be a forward or center? Auerbach had seen Dave in only one game. That was during Cowens' senior year at Florida State. Actually, Auerbach didn't even see one game. After only one half, he was convinced of Dave's ability. Auerbach didn't stay for the second half.

Auerbach has recalled watching Cowens. "He scared me the first time I scouted him. He was so good I kept hoping he'd make a mistake. There were scouts from half-a-dozen other NBA teams there that night. I figured if

they saw the same potential in Cowens that I did, I was dead."

Dave had become used to being overlooked. He came late to basketball. He was an unorthodox left-hander as a boy. He devoted most of his high school days in Newport, Kentucky, to swimming. This is not the way to attract college basketball scouts' attentions.

Hugh Durham was the Florida State coach. He struck it lucky. "I sent a lot of postcards to high school coaches," Durham has recalled. "Dave's coach at Newport Catholic answered. The coach said Cowens wasn't a great scorer, but could rebound. That was what we needed."

Cowens got little publicity playing at Florida State. The team won no national championship. Cowens didn't even make many of the All-American teams. One must remember, however, the others who were playing center in college at the time. There were Bob Lanier, Wesley Unseld, and Elvin Hayes. There was also a fellow named Lew Alcindor, who led UCLA to three straight national titles. Later he changed his name to Kareem Abdul-Jabbar.

Four years after Durham went shopping for a rebounder by mail, Auerbach was looking for the same thing. Auerbach's fear that others would see great potential in

Dave were unfounded. Dave was still there when the Celtics turn came to draft in the first round of the NBA draft.

Auerbach picked Cowens and signed him. It was a reported three-year, $300,000 contract. After the signing, Red breathed a sigh of relief. His choice was not to prove disappointing. Dave quickly made Auerbach look like a genius.

In his first year in Celtic green, Dave ran away with the Rookie of the Year award. He beat out better known players such as Lanier and Pete Maravich. Dave's 15 rebounds a game was the sixth best average in the league. He also averaged 17 points a game.

He upped those figures the following season. He scored almost 19 points a game. He averaged just over 15 rebounds each time out. This was fifth best in the NBA.

Dave established himself as a star in his third year. He averaged 20 points a game. He was third in the league in rebounding with a 16.2 average. His efforts were recognized. He was named the Most Valuable Player in the NBA for the 1972-1973 season.

Something more important to a team player like Dave was coming up. In 1973-1974 Boston won the NBA championship. It was the Celtics' first title since 1968-1969. The title drive was led by Dave and veteran John Havlicek. Dave's season scoring average of 19 points a game was second only to Havlicek on the Celtics.

No Boston player came close to matching Dave in rebounding. His 15.7 rebounds per game was second best in the entire league. He had over 300 more rebounds than any other Celtic.

Dave's value to the Celtics can easily be seen by looking at the club's performance without him. Boston was first forced to play without him for any length of time at the start of the 1974-1975 season. Dave missed the first 17 games because of a broken foot. The team struggled to a 9-8 record.

Upon Dave's return, the Celtics won 51 of their next 65. Winning almost 80 per cent of your games is a great record in pro basketball. The Celtics won the Atlantic Division. Their record tied them with the Washington Bullets for the best winning percentage in the NBA.

Unfortunately for the Celtics, the Bullets took them out of the play-offs. But Dave had the second highest scoring average of his pro career. He again finished second in the league in rebounding.

Writers and broadcasters in NBA cities named him to the All-Star second five. He finished second in the players' voting for the league's Most Valuable Player. He was named to the All-Defensive team's second team for the first time. His fine play also set the stage for the 1975-1976 season.

Cowens and Paul Silas controlled both backboards in 1975-1976. The Celtics won the Atlantic Division by eight games. The Celtics beat Buffalo and Cleveland to gain the championship series. Their opponents were the surprising Phoenix Suns.

The Suns battled back after losing the first two games in Boston. They won twice in Phoenix to tie the series. Those who saw the fifth game in the Boston Garden or on television will never forget that game. It took three over-times for the Celtics to edge the Suns, 128-126. Dave fouled out before the finish. He sat down with 26 points and a game-high 19 rebounds.

The Suns could now lose no more if they were to win their first NBA title. Dave's value to Boston was clearly seen in the sixth game. After picking up five fouls — one more would force him to the bench — he never eased up. Late in the game, he slapped away a Phoenix pass. He recovered the ball and dribbled the length of the court. He faked the lone defender off balance. Then he went to the hoop and made a driving, reverse lay-up. Fouled on the play, he sank the free throw.

The three-point play finished Phoenix. Boston won its 13th NBA title in 20 years. Dave had 21 points in the game. He once again was a game's top rebounder.

He had averaged 16 rebounds a game during the regular season. Again he was number two man in the NBA. Teammate Silas was fourth. Dave's season scoring average was 19 points.

Boston fans eagerly awaited the 1976-1977 season. They were convinced the Celtics could repeat as champions. They believed this even though the NBA had added four new teams and several star players from the disbanded ABA. Denver, Indiana, the New York Nets, and San Antonio were merged into the NBA in early summer. The best players on other ABA teams were claimed in a draft.

The 1976-1977 season did not start well for the Celtics. After a long contract dispute, Silas was traded to Denver. Paul was a fan favorite and one of Dave's closest teammates. The trade was part of a three-way deal that brought Curtis Rowe to Boston from Detroit. Boston then got Sidney Wicks from Portland to help offset the loss of Silas.

There was a problem molding the new players into the team. This process always takes time. It is especially so on a club that relies so heavily on the team concept. The Celtics struggled through the early season.

Then, in November, Dave shook the NBA with his announcement. The reaction, as he probably had feared, was predictable. Many questioned his sanity. A few cheered him and wished him well.

What bothered the first group was obvious. What normal player, they asked, would walk away from a $280,000 salary? Who would leave a team thought to have a good chance to win the NBA title?

Red Auerbach was not one who asked these questions. He knew that Dave was hardly the normal player. Dave's success resulted as much from his mental attitude as from his physical skill. His dedication and intensity were just as important as his speed and strength. Auerbach knew that Dave's mental attitude was important. If it was not right, the rest of his game would suffer.

Auerbach did not rant and rave. Many had expected such a reaction. Instead he told Dave that the team needed him. But he said the team would try to get along without him until Dave felt he could play as he thought he should.

Dave's leave of absence did not work out as he had hoped. He put 6,000 miles on his van. He spent some time in Boston and New York. He went to Florida. He was in Houston and other places. He spent some days over the Christmas holidays with his family in Cold Spring, Kentucky. He even watched a few Celtics games.

Still, it wasn't what he wanted. There is glitter and glamor that surrounds the professional athlete. The better the player, the more of this is present. Dave had always disliked this. He did not dress the part of the superstar. He preferred jeans and flannel shirts to stack heels and mink coats.

Earlier in his career, he had come to practice in greasy overalls. He loved cars and had been taking a course in auto mechanics.

He did not live the role of a superstar. He preferred a small house on the edge of a suburban estate to the city's bright lights.

"I like it out here," he had once said in explanation. "It's peaceful and it allows me to be myself. I can lead my life as I see fit. I'm not one for crowds. I don't like a great deal of noise. There is not much privacy for someone six-nine with red hair."

The life in a fish bowl he had been leading did not go away when he left the team. It grew worse. He became even more of a celebrity. What he had done kept reporters constantly after him. They wanted the answers to two questions. One was, "Why had he left?" The other was, "When would he return?"

Meanwhile, Auerbach kept in touch with Dave. The general manager applied gentle pressure. He wanted Dave to change his mind.

All of these things finally had their effect. Dave announced on January 12, 1977, that he would end his leave of absence. He would return to the Celtics after missing 30 games.

"I wanted to stay out the entire year," Dave told reporters. "I wanted to return at training camp next season. But I couldn't do it. It came to the point that I felt the best thing for me is to play . . . . If I didn't, I would be denying myself the privilege of doing what I do best."

Without Dave, the Celtics had managed to stay in the race for the play-offs. The team had a 4-4 record when he had left 65 days earlier. They were still struggling along at .500 when he returned. They were 19 and 19.

Merely having Dave back did not end Boston's problems. Guard Charlie Scott broke a wrist the day Dave agreed to return. The Celtics regained one starter, but lost another.

Cowens seemed different when he rejoined the Celtics. He appeared to have rediscovered the spark and fire that drove him. He played only 21 minutes in his first game back. Boston lost to Portland, 107-92. Dave got eight points and six rebounds. He fouled out with nine seconds to play. But at one point he chased down a loose Portland pass. He saved the ball and charged into the third row of seats, scattering fans.

This was the Dave Cowens who Boston fans had grown to know and love.

The Celtics again had to learn to adjust to changing personnel. They began to jell during the last part of the season. Scott came off the injury list April 3. The final week of the regular season remained for the Boston starting five to mesh. A week later the Celtics finished second in the Atlantic Division with a 44-38 record. They trailed Philadelphia by six games. However, they were in the play-offs.

The Celtics took San Antonio out of the play-offs in two straight games. Cowens brought smiles to the faces of Boston fans merely by playing like Dave Cowens.

The night after Boston's opening round dismissal of San Antonio, a Boston Globe reporter hailed a taxi. When he entered the cab, he saw that his driver was a 6-foot,

9-inch redhead. Recognized, Dave admitted to his passenger only that "I'm a basketball player. Other than that, leave me alone."

Dave knew it wouldn't end there. He had a friend who worked for the Boston Herald American. He didn't want the Globe to have a scoop. He told the story to his friend. Dave explained that he had wanted a way to relax. He thought driving a cab might be a different way to do it. "I just wanted to drive around the city," Dave told his friend. "I've ridden in a lot of cabs. I wanted to see what it would be like to drive one."

The friend also reported that the one-night job had cost Dave 50 dollars. There was 17 dollars for a three-year Boston taxi license. The cab rental was 25 dollars. Gasoline cost him 8 dollars. Dave also had said he had picked up only six passengers. Only one of his fares had recognized him.

The latest Cowens' escapade left basketball fans shaking their heads in wonder. Meanwhile Dave and the Celtics were ready to face Philadelphia in the first game of the Eastern semifinals.

Boston upset the favored 76ers in that first game. Dave scored 21 points in the 113-111 win. Three other Celtics had 20 or more in the nationally televised contest. The 76ers took the lead in the series by winning the next two games. Then, in game four, Dave went on a rampage.

In just the first half, he scored 23 points. He made every shot he took from the field — 10 of 10. He also grabbed 13 rebounds. He ended up playing a full 48 minutes for the first time all season. His game totals were 37 points and 21 rebounds. The Celtics evened the series at two games apiece. It was Dave Cowens at his best and most intense.

However, he couldn't lead his team to a 14th NBA title. The Celtics took the 76ers to the full seven games. But Philadelphia won the final game on its own court, 83-77. It was only the second time in 13 times over the years when Boston went to a seventh game in a play-off series that they were beaten.

There was some consolation for Boston fans. Cowens had played as he was capable of playing in the nine play-off games. He averaged almost 17 points and just under 15 rebounds a game. He also provided vital spark and leadership. This was the style that had earned him his reputation. The future looked solid for the Celtics. Dave was back. The players had begun to blend together on the floor. Hopefully, the injuries would not repeat.

There is always, though, the question. How long will basketball be able to hold Dave's attention? His leave of absence showed how much his other interests concern him.

Even before the 1976-1977 season, he had thought about retirement. What would he do after his days as a player? He had thought, it had been reported, about returning to farming, going back to Kentucky where his parents and family live. There was criminology, which he had studied at Florida State.

He also liked working with kids. He could try coaching on the high school level. Then there was his love of cars. It was said he had even considered opening a service station. Here he could put to use his study of auto mechanics.

Whatever the choice, the decision certainly seemed closer than it had before.

For the near future, his age and skills seemed to demand a few more seasons in the NBA. He turned 30 on October 25, 1978. This is not quitting age for most basketball stars. To leave early would deny him "the privilege of doing what I do best."

Dave Cowens at his best is enough to turn other pro centers green — with envy.

Football
Johnny Unitas
Bob Griese
Vince Lombardi
Joe Namath
O. J. Simpson
Fran Tarkenton
Roger Staubach
Alan Page
Larry Csonka
Don Shula
Franco Harris
Terry Bradshaw
Chuck Foreman
Ken Stabler

Baseball
Frank Robinson
Tom Seaver
Jackie Robinson
Johnny Bench
Hank Aaron
Roberto Clemente
Mickey Mantle
Rod Carew
Fred Lynn
Pete Rose

Basketball
Walt Frazier
Kareem Abdul Jabbar
Wilt Chamberlain
Jerry West
Bill Russell
Bill Walton
Bob McAdoo
Julius Erving
John Havlicek
Rick Barry
George McGinnis
Dave Cowens
Pete Maravich

superstars!
superstars!
superstars
superstars

CREATIVE EDUCATION SPORTS SUPERSTARS

Golf
Lee Trevino
Jack Nicklaus
Arnold Palmer
Johnny Miller
Kathy Whitworth
Laura Baugh

Miscellaneous
Mark Spitz
Muhammad Ali
Secretariat
Olga Korbut
Evel Knievel
Jean Claude Killy
Janet Lynn
Peggy Fleming
Pelé
Rosi Mittermaier
Sheila Young
Dorothy Hamill
Nadia Comaneci

Hockey
Phil and Tony Esposito
Gordie Howe
Bobby Hull
Bobby Orr

Tennis
Jimmy Connors
Chris Evert
Pancho Gonzales
Evonne Goolagong
Arthur Ashe
Billie Jean King
Stan Smith

Racing
Peter Revson
Jackie Stewart
A.J. Foyt
Richard Petty